ENCOUNTERING THE HOLY

ENCOUNTERING THE HOLY

An Advent Devotional

Sarah Katreen Hoggatt

Encountering the Holy: An Advent Devotional

ISBN: 978-0-9729460-6-3

Spirit Water Publications
P.O. Box 7522
Salem, OR 97303

All biblical quotations are taken from the *New International Version* unless otherwise noted.

Cover Photograph by Sarah Katreen Hoggatt
Cover Design by Sarah Katreen Hoggatt
Author Photograph by Stephen Custer, Dry Humor Marketing

Manufactured in the United States of America

CONTENTS

Introduction   vii

Daily Devotions

Hide and Go Seek with God   1

Peeking Through Our Window   2

Dancing Star!   3

The Light of God Within   4

Lessons from the Ages   5

The Lifeblood of Love   6

Singing Songs of Joy   7

A Time for Peace   8

Waiting for Christmas   9

What is Goodness Anyway?   10

Do I Have to Have Self-Control?   11

Everlasting Faithfulness   12

Pass It On   13

A Gentle Whisper   14

An Unfamiliar Voice   15

Staircase to God   16

Celebrate!   17

No Greater Love than This   18

Christmas Aromas   19

Sheets   20

Hanukkah   21

You Did This for Me   22

A Real Tree for Christmas   23

Why the Manger?   24

Holding the Messiah   25

Shepherds in the Dark   26

Simeon's Moment   27

And They Followed a Star...   28

O' Holy Night   29

INTRODUCTION

I remember as a high school student singing in a Christmas musical at church. One of the songs that has stayed with me ever since went something like this: "Got to get a gift, got to get a good gift, got to do my Christmas shopping! Got to get it here, got to get it there, not enough time for stopping! Come next year, one thing's clear, my shopping will be done. I'll start in January so Christmas will be fun!" These lyrics were accompanied by a crowd of people running around the stage with shopping bags, comparing with each other hideous gifts they had bought for their friends. This picture would be enormously amusing if it wasn't so true, if this frenzy isn't what we see every year when people realize Christmas is just a few weeks away.

I admit, I am guilty along with the rest when I realize how close Christmas is and knowing I have hardly even started thinking about Christmas surprises for my family and friends. Then in the midst of all that stress when we think over the list of to-do's, we all start to wonder, what are we doing this for, every year? The holidays are stressful and can be draining on our finances. Wouldn't it be better to not celebrate Christmas, to just let it be another day? That would make sense, if presents are what Christmas is all about, which, of course, it's not.

Christmas is about the over-arching and all-encompassing love with which we give those gifts. It's about the holy One who lives inside us, moves among us, and inspires our giving in the first place. It is about the One who loves us so deeply he gave us the best gift of all: himself amongst us. He gave us his time, his energy, he gave us his passionate embrace. Yet every year when we celebrate Christmas, we do everything but celebrate him. We celebrate our families, good food, presents, and beautiful decorations but we forget to give to the one who gave us all he had. We all too often neglect encountering the holy.

But what do you give the God who has everything? Maybe Jesus would like a new prayer shawl. Perhaps he would enjoy that book you saw on camel care the other day, or even better yet, bobble-heads of all the saints. He is such a difficult person to shop for. But is he really? After all, why was he born if not for his wish to be in relationship with us? We are the ones he wants: our time, our thoughts, space to be together. Why do we work so hard on finding the perfect gift for everyone else and don't give anything to the one we're celebrating?

One of the reasons I treasure this time of Advent every year is it reminds me to make sure I have time with God. It helps bring to mind my need to create open space where my Creator and I can talk, listen, enjoy each other's company, have space where I remember I am whole. I want to share in the silences with him, that quiet center at the core of myself where I hear what God says beyond the words, beyond language when only the soul understands. Especially at this time of year, when so much else is competing for attention, I need that reminder to keep making space for the one we're waiting for.

Advent, by definition, is the period in the Christian calendar when we await Jesus' birth, we wait to encounter the Holy One of Israel. This usually starts on the fourth Sunday before December 25th, thus it changes from year to year. Because this is a book, I wanted people to be able to read it year after year, Thus I decided to write devotions for the four weeks before Christmas starting on November 26th and going through to December 24th. The words are meant to be savored day by day, held, and pondered in open space. Talk about what you are reading with God, what meaning it holds for you. In addition to your time, you should listen for what he wants to give back to you within that time and beyond. Perhaps like Mary, something new will be born in you, maybe like Simeon, you will see a long-held dream come true. Perhaps there are seeds, qualities of character or new insights God is growing inside of your heart and you don't even know they are there.

Enjoy the holidays. Celebrate! Such festivity is a gift from God and they can be a lot of fun, but we need to remember the parties and the gifts, even time with family, are not the main focus of the season. The celebrations, the traditions, are reminders, the outer trappings of an inner reality. At their best, Christmas traditions are ways of creating room for us to encounter God, they are the holy places pointing to him.

Tonight, kneel down, light a candle. Remember who you were made for, remember the one who loves you beyond measurable worth. He came here to seek you out, now it is your turn to create the space, take the time, and seek him.

Sarah Katreen Hoggatt

November 26th

"But if from there you seek the LORD your God,
you will find him if you look for him
with all your heart and with all your soul."
Deuteronomy 4:29

Hide and Go Seek with God

It is a funny picture to imagine: God playing hide and go seek with us, hiding behind a rock or up a tree while we wander around looking for him. I think he must have to work hard on stifling his laughter as we call out. I think it must be difficult for him to resist popping out from behind that rock and yelling, "Surprise!" to our startled faces, just to catch our delight in finding him at last. I believe he would enjoy walking right behind us as we looked then grabbing us out of the blue. It would be hard for him to be away from us as we searched. Still, God is an excellent hide and go seeker as he can hide in, on, underneath, or above anything at all.

As you walk through your day today, start looking for him in the natural world around you. Perhaps it is while you are picking out a Christmas tree or taking a walk through the woods. Look behind those rocks, up those trees. Go ahead, stop and smell the pine, the clean wind-swept air. Can you sense God in the aroma? Can you see him floating in the lake or walking through the muddy field? Can you hear him singing on the mountain? He's there; all we have to do is look for him. It doesn't take much time but it will make worlds of difference in your awareness of his presence here with us. So go ahead, look…

November 27th

"For to see your face is like seeing the face of God."

Genesis 33:10

Peeking Through Our Window

As I write, there is a little boy peeking through my window. I don't know who he is, or why he is looking in here, but it makes me wonder. If God were to press his face against my window, would I notice? Would I consider it an annoying disruption or would I grin, wave back, and enjoy the curiosity on his face? What would the moment bring me? How would my life be changed if I saw God peeking through my window?

There are all kinds of people we come across in our lives. Some we just meet for a second, like the car wash attendant or a bank teller, some we are honored to journey with as companions for a time such as our friends and our families. Some bring us great joy and some bring us pain, but God is in them all. We are each a reflection of him for each other, we each show him in a different light. Some of us show his kindness best, others, his creative spirit. Then there are some who when we are around them, we feel beloved and at peace. You see, God is everywhere. He is peeking through the windows of the faces that surround us in our everyday lives. Today, look for the ways God is reflecting himself into your life in order to show you more of who he is and to help you grow closer to him. Who do you see peeking through your window?

NOVEMBER 28TH

"Do not be afraid, little flock,
for your Father has been pleased to give you the kingdom."

Luke 12:32

Dancing Star!

On my bulletin board at home is a purple ribbon with the words, "Dancing Star!" written in sparkling letters. It was given to me one summer afternoon last year when I was called up from the audience to learn a dance you could do with your hands. The experience, though stretching as it was in front of a *large* audience, was fun as it showed me more of what I could do and who I could be.

I think many times in our lives, God brings us experiences to help us learn and grow. He wraps them up, ties a ribbon, and hands the gifts to us with the words, "You can do it, I believe in you!" It can seem daunting at first as what he is asking of us is beyond anything we have yet done. But he, more than anyone else, knows he has prepared us for just such a moment as this and that this moment will prepare us for others yet to come.

To what moments is he calling you? Where is he moving in your life? What experiences is he bringing along your way? Pay attention to them, for in times like that, he is working within you. Then as you take that new step, do not worry, he will give you the courage to face your fears and to be transformed.

"By day the LORD directs his love,
at night his song is with me—
a prayer to the God of my life."

Psalm 42:8

The Light of God Within

When is the last time you looked in a mirror? If you are like most people, it probably wasn't that long ago, most likely, this morning at least. But did you really see yourself? You may have seen what you thought you looked like, but did you really see? Sure, you may have seen your hair, your nose, and that annoying pimple that just won't go away, but did you really see who you were? Did you really see the essence of you? God did. God looks at you every day and sees himself. When is the last time you did the same? When is the last time you came close enough to see his light reflected in your eyes? When is the last time you looked in the mirror and saw him smiling back at you? He is always there for he lives in you. He shines out from you and I will bet you a lot more people see him in you than you think. Isn't it time you started seeing him in yourself? It is one of the greatest gifts he's given you—his life always out flowing from the inner sanctuary of your soul. So next time you go up to a mirror to look at yourself, take a closer look and see what, or who, you can see.

November 30th

"O my people, hear my teaching;
listen to the words of my mouth.
I will open my mouth in parables,
I will utter hidden things, things from of old—
what we have heard and known,
what our fathers have told us."

Psalm 78:1-3

Lessons from the Ages

A few days ago, I attended a Jewish service for Yom Kippur at my local temple. The Rabbi read to us the story of Jonah and asked us questions of why we did this or that or why we are feeling what we are feeling as if we were the characters in the story themselves as it progressed. It made me think and once more, put me back into the Bible story, bringing it to life anew.

It amazes me how stories can play themselves out again and again in our lives, teaching us new insights every time. God speaks to us through such stories, revealing his character, insights into our lives, and tells us things he wants to do in our hearts. It is his way of inviting us further into himself, further into his truth and unspeakable grace. It is his way of giving you the courage to keep going when you know someone else has already done it.

What stories are playing out in your life? What truths inherent in them are reverberating in your thoughts? How do you see your life reflected in the story? Stories are indeed powerful things, how is God speaking through them to you?

DECEMBER 1ST

"But I am like an olive tree
flourishing in the house of God;
I trust in God's unfailing love
for ever and ever."

Psalm 52:1

The Lifeblood of Love

Have you ever noticed how a person starts blooming when they know they are loved? Like a wilted rose bush, a person can be dried up and emotionally frail but when another spreads the water of love around their roots of self-hood, the leaves come back to life and rosebuds start sprouting everywhere you look. Vines grow where there was no life before and the abundant flowers face themselves toward the sun.

God created love to be our lifeblood. We need it to survive even as much as flowers need water. We need God to show himself to us, to share with us who he is and to tell us how much he loves us even as he teaches us to say how much we love him. His love frees us to be ourselves for who cares about other's opinions of us when God is ecstatic about hearing ours? He loves every detail of who we are right down to our toes. He created them and the only things he creates are masterpieces.

I think this is the main reason Jesus came to this earth: to show us how much he loves us and to teach us how we can express our love back to him, to ourselves, and to each other. So where are you nurturing love in your life? What flowers need your attention? Give them some water and as God has done with you, watch them bloom.

DECEMBER 2ND

"Sing for joy, O heavens, for the LORD has done this;
shout aloud, O earth beneath.
Burst into song, you mountains,
you forests and all your trees,
for the LORD has redeemed Jacob,
he displays his glory in Israel."

Isaiah 44:23

Singing Songs of Joy

I love to sit down at a piano and play Christmas carols—any time of the year. I even have a music book with simple notes so it is easy for me to play them, and the words are written out so I can sing along. There is just something about singing and playing these old favorite tunes at Christmas that gives me joy.

Joy is defined as "to rejoice" and "a source or cause of delight". At Christmas, our cause of delight is not supposed to be the sparkling lights, the brightly wrapped presents, or even the family who often come over for dinner. Our delight is in a baby who was born, in the incarnate God who came to live amongst his people. Everything else about Christmas serves to remind us of him. The lights remind us of his light, the gifts bring to our mind the gift he is to us, and our families teach us how to live in fellowship with the Trinity and with each other.

It is in celebration of these deeper truths we sing for joy. Even if there are no presents, electricity costs too much to put up the lights, and our families don't get along, we will always have cause for delight as we raise our voices with the mountains in celebration of a tiny baby born on a starry night. So no matter your circumstances, celebrate with joy! God has come to live amongst us! What greater gift is there?

DECEMBER 3RD

"'I have seen his ways, but I will heal him;
I will guide him and restore comfort to him, creating praise on the
lips of the mourners in Israel. Peace, peace, to those far and near,'
says the LORD. 'And I will heal them.'"

Isaiah 57:18-19

A Time for Peace

For many people, this season is a hard one to "get in the spirit of." Perhaps this is their first Christmas without someone they loved, maybe their family is wrought with tension, it could be a difficult year financially, or it may be they are single and have no "family" to share the season with. In all of these situations and many more, peace can be in short supply as they walk through their grief. Their experience just doesn't match up with the classic picture of the family all around the Christmas tree. Peace is not a gift they expect to receive this year. But to give peace to such as these is precisely why Jesus was born.

What about "Jesus with us" gives us peace? Why does a crying baby change things for all time? We sing songs about peace for all people but rarely do we search out what we mean. But it is because of this day, we can all be at peace. Peace with God is knowing he is greater than any grief, his presence more overwhelming than any loneliness, and his love deeper than any poverty of spirit we could ever have. Peace is knowing God with us, Emmanuel, and because he is with us, because once more, he walks with us in the garden at the cool of the day, we can tell him of our grief, our pain, and our loneliness. Perhaps it is the broken-hearted who find the true spirit of the season, true peace, most of all.

DECEMBER 4TH

"Be patient, then, brothers, until the Lord's coming. See how the farmer waits for the land to yield its valuable crop and how patient he is for the autumn and spring rains. You too, be patient and stand firm, because the Lord's coming is near."

James 5:7-8

Waiting for Christmas

Advent is a whole season about waiting. We're waiting for the turkey dinner, for presents to be unwrapped, and to spend time with our friends and family. As we wait, we also prepare. We decorate our homes, go shopping, send out cards, and tell the story to each other of how God came to be with us. But it can be so hard to wait. Just ask the six-year-old who sees a gift for him under the tree three weeks before Christmas. So why does God make us do it? Why do we have to wait?

I love a phrase in Luke's gospel, "While they were there, the time came for the baby to be born." Mary had to wait. It wasn't an idle waiting though. The baby was growing, Mary and Joseph went on a road trip to Bethlehem, and I am sure throughout both, Mary prayed a great deal. So many times when we find ourselves waiting, we think it is a waste of time. Why can't we just have what we want right now? But God knows if he gave us what we wanted when we wanted it, we wouldn't be ready for it. We have to wait and prepare. We have to be patient knowing God's timing is perfect though we may not always see it. Patience is being at peace with where we are and knowing what is to come will indeed come, but we have to wait. Jesus had to wait too, thirty years he had to wait. He knows what it is like to have to be patient but he also knows that what comes to those who wait is far better than what they could find on their own. So be patient, prepare for what is to come, and wait. He is coming.

DECEMBER 5TH

"His divine power has given us everything we need for life and godliness through our knowledge of him who called us by his own glory and goodness."

2 Peter 1:3

What is Goodness Anyway?

Goodness is spoken of several times in the Bible. Have you ever wondered what it means? Simply put, I think it means our faith put into action in our daily life. It is the way God's light shines through us into the lives of others. Goodness is realizing we live for more than just ourselves, our wants and needs. Life is only truly lived when we look to the wants and needs of others.

Have you ever done something for someone else and felt lighter because of it? Have you ever gone out of your way to lend a hand and felt better about the life you've lived? I sure have! It seems to be the times when I've helped lighten someone else's load, my own has been lifted. I think it is because when we help another person, we gain a larger perspective of the world around us. We come to see we play a part in God's creation and it is through that knowledge of our creatureliness that we learn how to live out the characteristic of goodness in our own lives. What is more, God gives us the strength to do so. We need not rely on our own resources of goodness for after all, goodness does not flow out of our hearts, but God's heart with us. It can't be forced. Goodness is something God draws you into through his love and through the lives of others. How is God calling you to goodness? How can you look beyond your own life and reach out into the life of another? How can you lighten someone else's load this Christmas season?

DECEMBER 6TH

*"For the grace of God that brings salvation has appeared to all men.
It teaches us to say 'No' to ungodliness and worldly passions, and to
live self-controlled, upright and godly lives in this present age,
while we wait for the blessed hope—the glorious appearing of our
great God and Savior, Jesus Christ."*

Titus 2:11-13

Do I Have to Have Self-Control?

For my last birthday, a friend gave me the new Josh Groban CD,
a new release I have been greatly anticipating. However, I was
working on a large project at the time and the only music I allowed
myself to listen to was a Broadway show I knew very well. While I
loved the show's music, I could tune it out if I needed to and I knew I
would be unable to do that with the Josh Groban CD. I had to exert
self-control. (Difficult though it was.)

Self-control can be a hard discipline to learn. So often, it is much
easier to do what we want instead of what we need. It is a process
of realizing God knows what is best for us and we have to decide to
follow his wisdom over what we think or we want to do. It's not always
pretty and people won't always agree with us, but we do it because it
is right. We do it because we have chosen to rely on God's direction.
He has been this way before, he knows where the pitfalls are, and he
sees things we do not. Then as we grow in wisdom, God teaches us
self-control and helps us make these decisions for ourselves.

One of my favorite phrases is about self-control: "Character is
not about what you want to do, but about what you choose to do."
God is within you, you know what you should and should not do;
listen to his voice for self-control does not lead to boredom, but true
freedom when you enjoy things at the proper time. His time.

DECEMBER 7TH

*"Your kingdom is an everlasting kingdom, and your
dominion endures through all generations. The LORD is faithful
to all his promises and loving toward all he has made. The LORD
upholds all those who fall and lifts up all who are bowed down."*

Psalm 145:13-14

Everlasting Faithfulness

Christmas seems to come along faster every year. It seems as
if it was summer just a few weeks ago and here it is, almost
Christmas. The stores have been decorated for some time now and
holiday concerts are already in full swing. No matter if we are ready
or not, whether we want it to be or not, Christmas is here again.

Christmas in some ways is like God. Both are very faithful to
keep coming to us despite how we are doing. Both do not depend
upon us for their existence. The calendar year has been here long
before us and will be here long after us. And God will be the same
God no matter who we are or what we do. He is faithful to all he
has made. He says he will keep the covenant, he will stay true to his
promises, and he will always love us. Aren't you glad he does? Aren't
you thrilled God's behavior doesn't depend on ours?

How do we exhibit this quality of faithfulness in our own lives?
Are we faithful to God even when we do not see what he is doing?
Do we trust in him though we may not understand? Are we faithful
to those we love? Faithfulness can be a hard quality to develop as it
requires deep trust in what we do not see. It can sometimes ask you
to go against what your instincts are telling you to do. But trust in
God. He is faithful and he will teach you to be faithful too.

DECEMBER 8TH

"It was I who taught Ephraim to walk,
taking them by the arms;
but they did not realize
it was I who healed them.
I led them with cords of human kindness,
with ties of love;
I lifted the yoke from their neck
and bent down to feed them."

Hosea 11:3-4

Pass It On

When I was in college, a woman from the church I was attending invited me over to her house for lunch after the service. I couldn't tell you what her name was nor could I pick her face out from a crowd, but what I do clearly remember is how her hospitality made me feel. As a college student, being invited into a home for a meal was a rare treat and I remember walking back to my dorm thinking how I could not repay her in kind. It was a freely given gift and all I could do was say thank you. I remember thinking that is what God does for us. He invites us to his banquet knowing we could never repay him but with a simple thank you. Yet he is so kind.

Years later, when I was living in a house, I invited several college students over for dinner. They asked if they could cook since they rarely had the opportunity to do so; they had so much fun making a delicious pasta dish! I don't know if they remember that night, I certainly do, but for myself, it was an opportunity to pass on the pleasure once given to me. That is what kindness is, giving pleasure to another who cannot repay you. God did that for us and we can do that for one another. Who has been kind to you in your life? How can you pass that on to another this holiday season?

DECEMBER 9TH

"Then a great and powerful wind tore the mountains apart and shattered the rocks before the LORD, but the LORD was not in the wind. After the wind there was an earthquake, but the LORD was not in the earthquake. After the earthquake came a fire, but the LORD was not in the fire. And after the fire came a gentle whisper. When Elijah heard it, he pulled his cloak over his face and went out and stood at the mouth of the cave."

1 Kings 19:11-13

A Gentle Whisper

There was a time in my life when spiritually, I felt like I was lying in a bed with a high fever in a quiet room with God sitting by my side holding my hand. He didn't demand I get better, or give me advice on what I should or shouldn't do. He was simply there, a gentle presence who loved me. There has never since been a time when I have come to know him better, no other time when I have become so intimately familiar with his voice, and it intrigues me that it wasn't in a majestic and loud moment, but over months when we hardly said a thing.

Of course, God can be in the earthquake and he can be in the fire, but I think we hear him best in the whisper. When someone whispers, we know it's important. We crane our necks to hear them, we make sure we catch and remember every word; we often try to confirm what they've said. God is much the same. He often speaks quietly, touches gently, listens attentively. Then when we can't speak anymore, he is gentler still as he sits by our side not saying a thing. Though sometimes, I think I've heard him quietly sing. What does he sing? Why don't you listen to his gentle voice and find out? The whisper is always there...

DECEMBER 10TH

"The man who enters by the gate is the shepherd of his sheep. The watchman opens the gate for him, and the sheep listen to his voice. He calls his own sheep by name and leads them out. When he has brought out all his own, he goes on ahead of them, and his sheep follow him because they know his voice."

Luke 10:2-4

An Unfamiliar Voice

Recently, I was house sitting for several animals, one of which was a cat who was supposed to come in at night. Though I would call for her every evening, she would never come to the sound of my voice. It may have been her name, but the voice was unfamiliar.

As we approach the day when God first came to earth in an unfamiliar voice, I am reminded how often God takes our image of who he is and expands it into another. He doesn't seem to like us to stagnate on an image of him. So as he shows us new images this Advent season, I wonder, how will we respond? Will we prefer to stay hidden in the darkness, in the cold, wet rain because we are scared of what he may have for us? Do we look at him with fear or do we trust him to bring us into warmth and light? He is holding the door of his house open, he is calling our name. He wants to feed us and bring us into an ever greater awareness of who he is. Where are you? Are you in the dark, coming up the stairs, or heading through the door? Where do you want to be and what do you need to hear from God to help bring you there? Ask him, and he will answer you. He is calling. Will you answer him?

DECEMBER 11TH

"Flowers appear on the earth;
the season of singing has come,
the cooing of doves
is heard in our land.

The fig tree forms its early fruit;
the blossoming vines spread their fragrance.
Arise, come, my darling;
my beautiful one, come with me."

Song of Solomon 2:12-14

Staircase to God

One afternoon this last summer I was walking a friend's dog when I came across a beautiful staircase carved into a hillside with a garden along the edges. It was one of those sights that could be easily missed but it captured my imagination as I pictured God waiting for me in a cool glen at the top. I wondered, what he would say to me if I found him there? Then I imagined he would simply invite me to be in that space with him. We wouldn't have to say anything, just being there together would be enough.

As we hurry from store to store in search of the "perfect" gift, have you thought about what gift you are giving to God? It is a tough question. What do you get for the God who has everything? You can give him your time. You can give him the most precious gift of just being with him, of being present to what he wants to say to you. That is all he really wants. So as you are shopping this Christmas, remember to look for those staircases, those invitations along your way that will bring you into his presence, then return the gift by giving him your time.

December 12th

*"Then all the people went away to eat and drink,
to send portions of food and to celebrate with great joy,
because they now understood the words
that had been made known to them."*

Nehemiah 8:12

Celebrate!

When I was a girl, every Christmas my sisters and I would pour over the J.C. Penney catalog. It wasn't the furniture or the clothes that interested us. No, it was the toys. There were pages and pages of wonderfully appealing things to play with and we wanted them all for Christmas! However, we never found them all under the tree on Christmas morning. And now looking back, where would we have put them all?

Life at Christmas can be a lot like that catalogue. There are so many wonderful things to do and ways to celebrate—caroling, baking, concerts, tree lightings, shopping sales, bazaars, but if we did them all, would we be awake enough to enjoy them? Where is the time to just enjoy the Christmas season and what it means for us? Without that sacred space and time filled with wonder and silence, what do we miss? How often do we get distracted by the trappings of Christmas, the gifts of the wise men and the singing of the angels, and forget to go see and worship the Christ child for ourselves?

Celebrations are wonderful and God has given them for us to enjoy. They are a way to *remember* what and who we value. But they do not constitute the *reason* we have joy. So while you are celebrating, give space to who you are celebrating for.

DECEMBER 13TH

*"There is no greater love than to lay
down one's life for one's friends."*

Luke 15:13 (NLT)

No Greater Love than This

Yesterday I was driving home and thinking about the verse above. I saw the faces of those for whom I would willingly lay down my life so they could live theirs. It was a startling thought to think of giving up my life for someone else. I had not thought a great deal on it before but I knew if it ever came to such a situation, I would make the choice to die in a heartbeat. It is through no virtue of my own, but that God has placed such a love in me for them, that it overcomes any fear I have about dying.

Being willing to die for someone though, doesn't have to actually end in death. There are all kinds of small ways we can give our lives to those we love. Look at the mother staying up late with a sick child, or the friend going out of their way to help another. It is the volunteers staffing the shelters and it is the stranger taking the extra time to smile at you as you pass by on the street. These are the small acts throughout the day given unselfishly and in love. They are as important as the final act of dying and I think just as valuable to the God we love. After all, isn't dying and living for someone we love what Christmas is all about? Isn't that why Jesus was born? So he could show us day by day a love greater than any we have ever known? So when you think about those you would die for, remember the one who already died for you and how he lived that love out every day of his life.

DECEMBER 14TH

"But thanks be to God, who always leads us in triumphal procession in Christ and through us spreads everywhere the fragrance of the knowledge of him. For we are to God the aroma of Christ among those who are being saved and those who are perishing."

2 Corinthians 2:14-15

Christmas Aromas

One of my favorite things about the Christmas season is the smell of baking. You know, when you walk into a house with the aroma of gingerbread cookies and hot apple cider laced with nutmeg, and a good dose of evergreen tree on the side? There is nothing in the world like it. It feels like coming home, all warm and cozy. Once you're in a house like that, it never seems to matter much what is going on outside, you are home.

I think that is how God wants us to feel with him in prayer, warm and safe within him. I think he enjoys inviting us in when we make the time to stop by. We might sit on the couch by the fire with a cup of hot eggnog in one hand and a cookie in the other. He asks us how we're doing, what is on our mind? We talk and he listens as we sit there and share with each other what is most precious to our hearts. We hear him tell of how he sees things and what he thinks of us; he asks us questions. However, even when at last we leave and go into other homes, his aroma stays with us. That scent of love and warmth is like the cloak he wrapped us in before we left, an aroma that clings to our beings as we interact with the world around us. Our presence will bring that same sense of peace and love we felt from him. God with us will help people to remember God with them as the aroma travels from one home to another.

December 15th

"As it is written:
'No eye has seen,
no ear has heard,
no mind has conceived
what God has prepared for those who love him.'"

1 Corinthians 2:9

Sheets

I remember one Christmas in particular when I was young when for weeks, or what seemed like weeks, our living room had been closed off with a sheet and we weren't allowed to go inside. As children, my sisters and I were extremely curious as to what was on the other side of that sheet and though I don't know how we did it, we managed to wait through those loooong days to find out. (I think my mother's stern eyes had something to do with it.) But finally, early on Christmas morning, we lined up in the hallway beside the sheet eager with anticipation. When it was at last taken down, we stepped in to find brand new bikes for each of us! I was thrilled and it didn't take me long to become a master on my bike, racing up and down our street without using my hands. (A talent I posses to this day.)

Metaphorically speaking, God put up a sheet for us as well. Not to keep us out of something, but to prepare his surprise for Christmas morning. Though he told us what he was doing, what mind could have fully conceived what, or who, was waiting for us? And just like my mom's gift, his was designed to bring us somewhere—into fellowship with the Trinity. Instead of making us pedal for ourselves though, he lifts us up onto the handlebars as my sister used to do with me, and he gives us the ride of our lives. It can be so hard to wait for what God brings us, but every time we do, we always discover what he gives us is worth the wait, Christmas most of all.

December 16th

"No one lights a lamp and puts it in a place where it will be hidden,
or under a bowl. Instead he puts it on its stand,
so that those who come in may see the light."

Luke 11:33

Hanukkah

Today as I write, it is the first day of the eight day celebration called Hanukkah. The holiday commemorates the miraculous event when after the temple was rededicated during the Maccabee revolution, a day's worth of consecrated oil burned for eight days until more could be made. To remember this, the Jewish people burn candles in a menorah, adding one candle for each day of Hanukkah. However they do not burn the candles to light the home within, but they put the menorah on a windowsill to light the world without.

I think there is a strong lesson for us to learn from the Hanukkah candles. The light of God within us is not there for ourselves. We are a light for each other. We are to be the menorah candles standing in the window; we are to be the ones reminding all who walk by of the glory of God and the great miracles he brings forth in the world. Just as the Jewish people always burn the candles for a certain amount of time after dark, so are we to be lights in the darkness of the night. One candle can make a huge difference in a darkened room. Just think what eight can do!

Another Hanukkah tradition is that each night when the candles are lit, the first blessing is said. "Praised are You, Lord our God, King of the Universe, who sanctified us with his commandments and commanded us to kindle the Hanukkah lights." May God command the lights within us to be lit as well.

December 17th

*"For I was hungry and you gave me something to eat,
I was thirsty and you gave me something to drink, I was a stranger
and you invited me in, I needed clothes and you clothed me, I was
sick and you looked after me, I was in prison and you came to visit
me.... I tell you the truth, whatever you did for one of the least of
these brothers of mine, you did for me."*

Matthew 25:35-36, 40

You Did This for Me

I think this verse has a lot to say to each of us. Not only does it give us ideas for things we can be doing, but it also tells us why we should do them. We believe God's light shines forth in each one of us no matter who we are. If we truly do see God's image in those around us, wouldn't we want to give them a drink, feed them, or visit them?

What also interests me about this verse is what it does not say. It does not say, "You gave me a barrel of water, a whole wardrobe, or let me stay in your house for years." Although those things are done and are good to do, it is not what God said. He said you gave me a drink, you visited me. All the things Jesus listed only costs a few dollars if anything and wouldn't take that long to do. For someone with my budget and schedule, yet still with the desire to serve, these words of Christ's are very uplifting. He doesn't ask us to only do the big things, but he urges us to do the small, the trivial, because he knows it is often the small things that make a world of difference.

It doesn't take me long to give someone a drink, or to watch over them when they are sick. After all, hasn't God already done that for me? Can't I do it for someone else? Can't we all?

DECEMBER 18TH

A Real Tree for Christmas

The first year I could have my own Christmas tree, I couldn't afford one so I set up a small fake tree I had bought years before and decorated that. However, I had a dream. I wanted a *real* Christmas tree for Christmas but financial prospects looked bleak so I made do with what I had. The day before Christmas Eve, a long-time friend was supposed to drop off a gift. The bell rang and I opened the door to a *real* Christmas tree on my front porch with two muffled voices behind it singing, "We Wish You a Merry Christmas!" While my friend's brother helped me get the tree inside the house, a sneaky elf was slipping things into my stocking and beneath the tree, things I didn't find until Christmas morning. Now, a few years and several real Christmas trees later, that is still the Christmas that makes me cry with joy.

We talk so much about the value of family during this time but not so much about the value of friends, those we would have chosen to have as family. They are the ones we choose to spend our time with, those with whom just being together brings great delight. Our friends are often the ones who lift us up when we need an encouraging word, or give us a hand when we need help. They are the ones God has placed in our lives to reflect his image. Though I know this can be a busy season between family and preparations, remember to take the time to enjoy your friends. They really are priceless people. And perhaps they too, need their version of a real Christmas tree this Christmas to brighten their lives. Would you please bring one?

December 19th

"She gave birth to her firstborn, a son.
She wrapped him in cloths and placed him in a manger,
because there was no room for them in the inn."

Luke 2:7

Why the Manger?

These last two weeks I have been in charge of feeding fifteen llamas every day. Every morning hay goes into their bins and every morning I have to step through what they leave behind. Though it is fun to see them and feed them in the early morning dawn, it strikes me anew what a dirty place in which Jesus must have been born. I wonder if Joseph felt bad about not being able to provide anything better? I wonder why God did not.

Of all the places Jesus could have been born in, why was it destined to be where animals were kept with everything that entails? Why not a nice clean room with at least a midwife present who could help Mary through her labor? What point did that make? Nothing is done without reason, why would God choose to place two people who said yes to his will in such circumstances? Why does God put us in such circumstances? Why, when we say yes to his will, does he place us in places filled with difficulty and even pain? I think it is the experience of difficulty that he values. He knows if we experience difficulty, we will be more approachable in the eyes of those around us. If Jesus had been born in a palace, the shepherds would never have been let in. If Jesus had been born "with a silver spoon in his mouth", those with wood would never have known him. What experiences in your life have made you more approachable in the eyes of others? What mangers have you been laid in lately? Perhaps it is time to see our mangers differently.

DECEMBER 20TH

*"Therefore the Lord himself will give you a sign: The virgin will be
with child and will give birth to a son, and will
call him Immanuel. [God with us.]"*

Isaiah 7:14

Holding the Messiah

Last spring, my sister gave birth to a daughter. Never before had
I seen a baby just after birth and it was an amazing experience.
Her feet were still a dark purple as oxygen hadn't reached them
yet and her mass of dark brown hair was still matted to her head.
Holding her, I marveled at how God brings new life into the world
and without even knowing who she was or would become, I loved
this little niece of mine with a great love.

I imagine that is just a tiny taste of what Mary and Joseph must
have felt when they first held Jesus in their arms. I am sure you who
are parents, have an even better sense of that feeling than I do. Can
you picture the scene? Can you picture Joseph placing Jesus in Mary's
arms and the marvel she felt as she not only held her son, but also the
Messiah whom her people had been waiting for? What amazement
she must have been filled with!

What amazes me even more than that picture is that Jesus is also in
each of us. He has placed himself within each living soul and though
we cannot always tell what he is doing, he is there, working, helping
us grow into greater fullness within him. What grace abounds in us,
what beauty lies within each of our hearts! Then what a miracle when
Jesus once again is birthed through us into the world, when we can
hold him and marvel at what God has done.

December 21st

*"And there were shepherds living out in the fields nearby, keeping
watch over their flocks at night. An angel of the Lord appeared to
them, and the glory of the Lord shone around them, and they were
terrified. But the angel said to them, 'Do not be afraid. I bring you
good news of great joy that will be for all the people. Today in the
town of David a Savior has been born to you; he is Christ the Lord.
This will be a sign to you: You will find a baby wrapped in cloths
and lying in a manger.'"*

Luke 2:8-12

Shepherds in the Dark

During a fierce storm one night while I was at my tap dancing
class, the lights in the studio went out. Though we found
ourselves tip-tapping in the dark without music, we weren't terribly
bothered by it since the emphasis was supposed to be on the sounds
of our taps anyway. In fact, we saw it as a great teaching tool. Since
we could only see vague shadows, we *had* to listen to each other. We
had to tune our ears to listen to the steps around us and in the dark,
come together.

I wonder if that is why the angels chose the shepherds with whom
to share the glorious news of the Messiah's birth. I wonder if it was
because since they had been sitting in the dark listening for potential
predators trying to harm their sheep that they could hear the angels
sing. Was it *because* of the darkness the angels came?

Oftentimes when we feel like we are living in the dark, we want
to fight against it and move into the light. But perhaps we are in
this place to hear something we would never have otherwise heard.
Perhaps God has placed us here to make sure we listen to him and
hear what he has to say. So when the lights go out and you can't see
what is around you, listen, for you too, may just hear the angels sing.

26

DECEMBER 22ND

"Simeon took him in his arms and praised God, saying: 'Sovereign Lord, as you have promised, you now dismiss your servant in peace. For my eyes have seen your salvation, which you have prepared in the sight of all people, a light for revelation to the Gentiles and for glory to your people Israel.'"

Luke 2:28-32

Simeon's Moment

There is a painting by Ron DiCianni titled, "Simeon's Moment." In the painting, Simeon's face shines with ecstasy as he holds the baby Jesus who he knows will one day redeem the world. What was going through his mind at that moment? It was a moment he had been waiting for his entire life. What did it feel like to finally live it? What did it feel like to know his greatest dream had been fulfilled in the form of a sleeping baby held in his arms? Did he laugh? Did he cry? What emotions rushed through his heart? When we hold Jesus, what emotions rush through ours?

It may seem strange to think we too can hold Jesus but we do it every day. When we hug a friend, hold a child, or kiss our spouse, we are holding Jesus all over again. It is a beautiful moment meant to be savored and enjoyed for just like Simeon's moment, it is fleeting. He did not get to hold Jesus for long. Still, this moment comes in many forms and it comes often. What moments are you waiting for? The Holy Spirit led Simeon to his and he will lead you to yours as well. Just remember, these moments often come unexpectedly, Simeon didn't know he would see the Savior that day. Neither do we. Keep listening, keep watching, and when the moment does come, savor it with everything you have.

27

DECEMBER 23RD

"After they had heard the king, they went on their way, and the star they had seen in the east went ahead of them until it stopped over the place where the child was. When they saw the star, they were overjoyed. On coming to the house, they saw the child with his mother Mary, and they bowed down and worshiped him."

Matthew 2:9-11

And They Followed a Star...

Can you imagine the conversation between the magi on the way to see Jesus? I imagine it went something like this: "Hey Ralph, did you remember to bring the frankincense? Yes, I see the star. No, we don't need to stop and ask for directions. I know exactly where we're going. This is just the scenic route." When they arrived, (Jesus was probably close to two years old by this time), they gave Jesus and his parents the gifts they had brought from afar. I wonder how long they stayed? If you had traveled for years to see someone, how long would you stay? Though the account in Matthew doesn't say, I would venture a guess they stayed at least several days. What was it like for them to see the King of the Jews toddle around? Was he what they expected or did he take them by surprise?

How often in our own lives do we follow the star toward who we think Jesus may be then are surprised when we get there? How often do we think we know what Jesus will look like but when we see him, have a hard time recognizing who he really is? We follow the star, we bring our gifts, we may have even gotten lost on the way, but what do we do when we get there? The wise men trusted the star and so bowed down and worshiped him. Let us do the same.

DECEMBER 24TH

"And you will sing
as on the night you celebrate a holy festival;
your hearts will rejoice
as when people go up with flutes
to the mountain of the LORD,
to the Rock of Israel."

Isaiah 30:29

O' Holy Night

My favorite Christmas carol begins with the lyrics, "O' Holy night, the stars are brightly shining. It is the night of our dear Savior's birth!" It reminds me of a crystal cold night with stars above emblazed, just waiting for that one moment when the world is forever changed. Tonight we all wait with bated breath for the Savior to come. Tonight Heaven and earth will kiss once again as Divine and human come together into one being for all time. It is a night of holy reverence, of awe-inspiring worship, of being able to touch the face of God.

What draws you to his side this night? Is it his humble beginnings, how he understands wherever you have come from? Is it the love in his eyes he holds for you as you come to his room to hold him? It may be you saw him in a place you didn't expect and want to know more or maybe you were told of him and so you left your sheep to come see what it was all about for yourself. For whatever reason you have come, the night is here, he is here, and he is here for you.

"Long lay the world in sin and error pining,
till he appeared and the soul felt its worth.
A thrill of hope the weary world rejoices,
for yonder breaks a new and glorious morn.
Fall on your knees! Oh hear the angel voices!
Oh night divine! Oh night when Christ was born!"

29

www.ingramcontent.com/pod-product-compliance
Lightning Source LLC
Chambersburg PA
CBHW060637030426
42337CB00018B/3390